Project Editor Sue Grabham
Senior Contributing Editor Charlotte Evans
Assistant Editor Tara Benson
Section Editor Angela Holroyd

Senior Designer Janice English
Staff Designer Sandra Begnor
Additional Design Smiljka Surla

Publishing Director Jim Miles

Art Director Paul Wilkinson

Additional Art Preparation
Matthew Gore, Andy Archer, Shaun Deal,
Julian Ewart, Narinder Sahotay, Andy Stanford,
Janet Woronkowicz

Picture Research Elaine Willis
Artwork Archivist Wendy Allison
Artwork Researcher Robert Perry

Activity Artist Caroline Jayne Church

Indexer Hilary Bird

Photo credits
14 Mansell Collection;
21 BATMAN is a trademark of
DC Comics ©1991. All Rights Reserved.
Reprinted by permission of DC Comics

Production Manager Linda Edmonds
Production Assistant Stephen Lang

Contributing Author Michael Chinery

Specialist Consultants
David Burnie BSc (Natural Sciences writer);
Julia Stanton BA DipEd (Australasia consultant)

Educational Consultants
Ellie Bowden (Curriculum Advisor for
Primary Science and Senior Teacher, Essex);
June Curtis (Primary School Teacher, Nottingham
and R.E. writer);
Kirsty Jack (Head Teacher, Primary
School, Edinburgh)

KINGFISHER
An imprint of Larousse plc
Elsley House, 24-30 Great Titchfield Street, London W1P 7AD

First published by Larousse plc 1994
Reprinted 1997

A CIP catalogue record for this book is available from the British Library

ISBN 0 7534 0151 7

Typeset by Tradespools Ltd, Frome, Somerset
Colour separation by P&W Graphics, Singapore
Printed in Hong Kong by
South China Printing Company (1988) Limited

KINGFISHER
Child's World

All Kinds
of
Animals

Kingfisher

Activities

Before you start each activity, collect everything you need and make sure there is a clear space. Remember to wear gloves when touching soil, and an apron for gluing, cooking and using paints. Use round-ended scissors for cutting, and if an adult is needed, ask if they can help before you start.

Afterwards, make sure you clear up any mess and put everything away.

▷ Here are some of the materials that you might need for the activities. **Always** ask an adult before using anything that is not yours.

You will find lots of exciting things in this book to do and make.

Before you start cooking
- put on an apron
- wash your hands
- ask an adult to be nearby if you are cooking with a saucepan, or to put the oven on for you if you are baking food.

All Kinds of Animals

What is an animal?

Animals are living things. So are plants. They both need energy to live, but they get their energy in different ways. Plants use the sun's energy. Animals cannot do that. Animals get their energy from the food they eat. Some animals eat plants, some eat other animals, and some eat plants and animals. There are many different kinds of animal. Scientists arrange them in groups.

the frog is an amphibian

the swallow is a bird

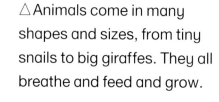
△ Animals come in many shapes and sizes, from tiny snails to big giraffes. They all breathe and feed and grow.

the mouse is a mammal

the cricket is an insect

Word box
Vertebrates are animals with backbones as part of their skeletons.
Invertebrates are animals without backbones. Some have a hard outside, a bit like armour. This is called an external skeleton.

the tortoise is a reptile

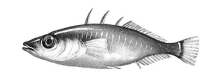
the stickleback is a fish

▽ These animals are all mammals. They are more closely related to each other than to birds or reptiles or fish. Can you find mammals on the chart below?

the fox is
a mammal

human beings
are mammals

the zebra is
a mammal

the panda
is a mammal

Tiny animals

Many animals are so small that we need a powerful microscope to see them.

animal under
a microscope

▽ There are over a million different kinds of animal. Scientists divide them into two main groups. Animals with backbones are called vertebrates. Animals without backbones are called invertebrates.

4,000
amphibians

4,150
mammals

6,500
reptiles

8,800
birds

21,500
fish

over
1 million

Vertebrates

Invertebrates

Animals in danger

The area an animal lives in is called its habitat. Today many of these habitats are in danger of being destroyed. The animals that live there will die. Some kinds of animal will become extinct, which means they will disappear for ever. This map shows some of the animals in most danger.

Noah's ark

The very old story of Noah's ark tells how one man and his family saved all the animals from a terrible flood. By finding out why the animals on this map are in danger you might be able to do something to help animals too.

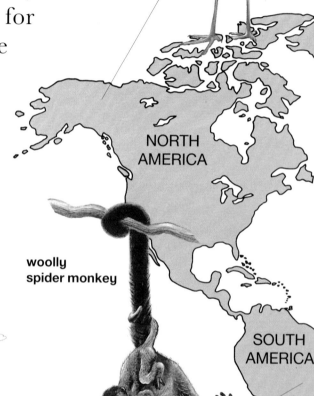

whooping crane

woolly spider monkey

NORTH AMERICA

SOUTH AMERICA

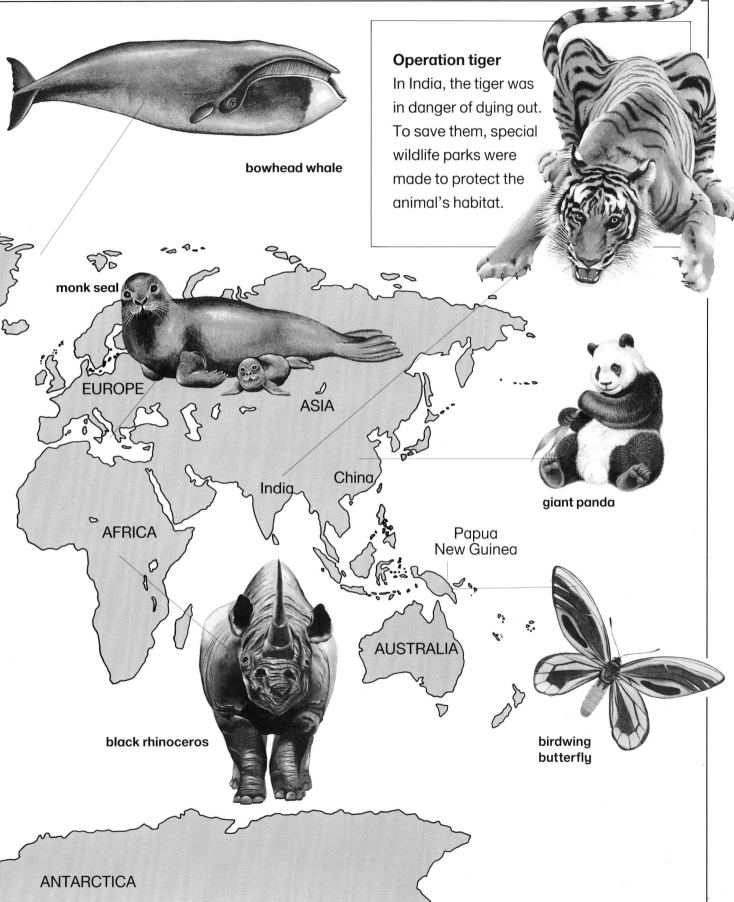

bowhead whale

Operation tiger
In India, the tiger was in danger of dying out. To save them, special wildlife parks were made to protect the animal's habitat.

monk seal

EUROPE

ASIA

giant panda

India

China

AFRICA

Papua
New Guinea

AUSTRALIA

black rhinoceros

birdwing
butterfly

ANTARCTICA

What is a mammal?

A mammal is an animal with hair or fur. This often helps to keep its body warm. Young mammals are fed with milk produced by their mother's body.

Mammals live almost everywhere, from freezing cold Antarctica to scorching hot Africa. Most mammals live on the land. Some, such as whales, live in water. Bats are the only mammals that can fly.

Find the answers

Which mammals can fly?

What do rabbits use their whiskers for?

We are mammals too
Human beings are mammals. We are fed with our mother's milk when young. All mammals are warm-blooded – their body temperature remains the same all the time, even though the temperature of their surroundings may change.

Word box
Herbivore is an animal that eats only plants.
Carnivore is an animal that eats other animals.

◁ Mammals often give birth to several young at once.

▽ Most mammals are good at seeing, hearing and smelling things around them. Rabbits use whiskers to feel things, too.

Design a mammal game

Each player think of a mammal. Draw its head at the top of a page. Fold over and pass onto next player. Draw the top half of the mammal's body, then its lower body and feet. Fold over and pass on each time. Open papers out to find new mammals.

hair or fur

whiskers

most mammals move on four legs

▷ Most mammals give birth to live babies, but the platypus lays eggs with leathery shells.

◁ Some mammals hibernate. They eat a great deal in the autumn, then curl up and sleep through the cold winter. This dormouse will not wake up until spring.

11

Monkeys and apes

Most monkeys and apes
spend a lot of time in trees,
so they need to be good at
balancing. They grasp things with
their hands, and use their arms and
legs to swing through the trees.

Apes are different from monkeys
because they do not have tails.
Gorillas are the largest of all
the apes.

△ The gibbon is an ape. With
its long arms, fingers and toes,
it is a good climber.

◁ This spider monkey is
using its strong tail, as well
as its hands and feet, to
hold onto the branches.

Pick up monkeys game
Trace the monkey template
onto stiff card. Cut out ten
monkeys. Players take turns to
pick up monkeys using the
arms and tails. The player who
makes the longest
chain wins.

▷ Baby monkeys
and apes are
carried by their
mothers until they
are old enough to
look after
themselves.

△Gorillas may look fierce, but they are shy and gentle. Like us, gorillas live in families, cuddle their babies and play together.

▷Apes are clever. This chimpanzee is using a stick to poke out tasty termites from their nest.

△Orang utans are apes. They like to live alone, but a mother always looks after her young.

13

Cats

All cats are meat-eaters. They use their good sight, hearing and sense of smell to hunt.

Cats have padded paws, so they can quietly creep up on another animal. Their long, sharp teeth and claws help to grip and kill it.

Alice's Adventures in Wonderland
(A story by Lewis Carroll)

Alice met some very strange characters in Wonderland. The Cheshire Cat slowly disappeared, starting with his tail, leaving his broad grin until last!

◁ Tigers are the biggest cats. They live in forests and grasslands.

▽ Some of the big cats are very fast. A cheetah is the fastest animal on land. Cats' long tails help them to keep their balance when they run and jump.

cat   wild cat   lynx   cheetah   leopard   black panther   lions

Living in a herd

Some mammals live in groups or herds. Herbivores, or plant-eaters, are safer in a herd. If one animal sees, hears or smells danger, it warns the rest. Some carnivores, or meat-eaters, hunt in groups called packs.

○ gaggle

● pride

● litter

● flock

geese

kittens

Find the animal groups
Each of these words describes an animal group. Follow the lines with your finger to find out which is which.

sheep

lions

▽ Wolves are carnivores that hunt in packs. Wolves work together to chase and corner a big animal.

Biggest of all

African elephants are the biggest land animals. They can grow as tall as three and a half metres and weigh as much as six tonnes. The biggest of all animals is a mammal that lives in the sea. The blue whale is the largest animal ever to have lived on Earth.

▽ The blue whale has no teeth, but has strips of whalebone called baleen. It eats tiny shrimps, called krill, which it filters out of the water through its baleen.

How the Whale got its Baleen
(Based on a story by Rudyard Kipling)

A whale swallowed a ship-wrecked man and his raft, but the man refused to be eaten. He made the whale take him home. The man wove his braces and raft together and pulled it into the whale's mouth to stop it swallowing anyone else. The whale could not spit it out, or swallow it, so it became his baleen.

▷Elephants live in herds. They use their trunks to take food and water to their mouths. They are strong enough to push trees over to get at the leaves.

Make elephant chains
Fold a long piece of paper into wide zigzags. Draw an elephant on the top of the paper. Make sure that the tail and trunk reach each side, as shown. Cut out the elephant shape and unfold to make an elephant chain.

△ Blue whales can be as long as six or more elephants.

17

Water mammals

Some mammals spend a lot of time in water. The hippopotamus lives in Africa and stays in the water to keep cool during the burning hot days.

Most seals live in cold water. They have a thick layer of blubber, or fat, which helps them stay warm.

Polar bears live in the Arctic. They are good swimmers. Their thick, white coats keep them warm.

▽ The hippopotamus usually leaves the water at night to feed on plants. Hippopotamus means water horse.

▽ Seals like to sunbathe on rocks. Their flippers make them excellent swimmers, but they are clumsy on land.

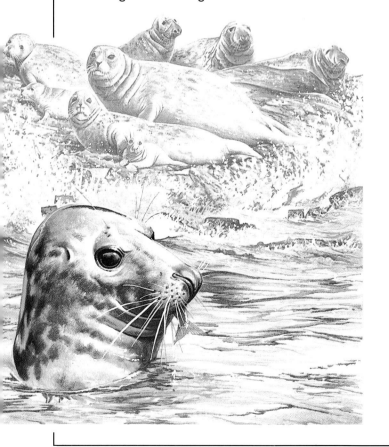

▷ Polar bears are large and fierce hunters. To catch a seal, a polar bear waits beside a hole in the ice until a seal comes up for air.

Busy rodents

Rodents are mammals with strong, sharp front teeth that they use to gnaw, or chew. Rodents gnaw at almost anything. Rats sometimes eat the walls of buildings.

▽ Beavers gnaw down trees to dam streams and make a lake. They build nests, called lodges, in the lake.

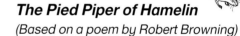

The Pied Piper of Hamelin
(Based on a poem by Robert Browning)

The townspeople of Hamelin promised a piper gold if he rid them of rats. He played his pipe, and the rats followed him to the river and drowned. But the town refused to pay him, so he played a new tune, and led away all the town's children to a new land.

▽ Marmots live in groups called colonies. They dig underground homes called burrows.

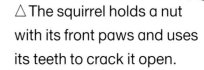

△ The squirrel holds a nut with its front paws and uses its teeth to crack it open.

19

Marsupials

Marsupials are mammals that have a pouch where their young grow. Baby marsupials are born very small. They crawl straight into their mother's pouch. Here they are kept safe while they feed on their mother's milk. When they are strong enough they leave the pouch.

▷ Wombats live in Australia. Marsupials live only in Australia and the Americas.

▽ Koalas are often called bears, but they are not real bears at all. They eat no meat, just eucalyptus leaves.

△ Kangaroos use their strong, thick tails to balance. Their babies are called joeys.

Make a kangaroo puppet

Stitch a pocket to the palm of a mitten. Glue on paper eyes, nose, ears and mouth.

Cut out and colour in a joey to fit in the pocket. Wear the puppet and bend your fingers to make a nose.

Bats

Bats are the only mammals that can fly. Their wings are folds of skin, stretched over long, thin fingers.

Many bats make high-pitched squeaks when they fly. The sounds bounce off objects all around them and they hear the echoes. This is how these bats find their way.

△ Bats sleep upside down in caves or trees. Most bats are nocturnal, which means they sleep in the day and hunt at night.

◁ Most bats eat insects such as moths. Some bats can snatch fish from the water with their feet.

Flying fox

Some bats eat fruit. A bat called the flying fox eats fruit. It is the largest bat of all.

Batman

Batman is a superhero who comes out at night, like bats do. He cannot fly, though. Batman drives around Gotham City in his batmobile.

What is a bird?

A bird is an animal with feathers and wings. Birds live in most parts of the world, and nearly all of them can fly.

The smallest bird is the bee hummingbird, which is only five centimetres long. The largest is the ostrich, which can grow to two and a half metres tall.

birds' ears are on either side of their head hidden by feathers

pigeon

The Ugly Duckling
(A story by Hans Andersen)

The cruel animals teased the Ugly Duckling for his ugliness. But by spring, he had grown into a beautiful swan.

Print a peacock
Using bright paints, make hand prints on paper. When dry, cut them out and glue in a fan shape to make a peacock's tail. Cut out a body and glue it in the middle of your picture.

Word box
Preening is the way a bird keeps itself clean. A bird preens its feathers with its beak.
Birds of prey are birds that hunt other animals for food.

beak or bill

Canada geese

△ When a bird flaps its wings, its feathers push the air back and down, so the bird moves forward and up.

birds have two feet with claws for gripping

ostrich

△ A few birds, such as the huge ostrich, cannot fly. But the ostrich can run very fast.

Feathers

Birds are the only animals with feathers. Feathers give birds their colours and help to keep them warm.

Birds often preen, or clean their feathers. They use their beaks to rub in oils from their body. Birds pull out old feathers where newer ones have grown.

◁ The tiny hummingbird beats its wings more than 60 times a second while it drinks nectar from flowers.

△ A flamingo's feathers are pink because it eats pink shrimps.

▽ The patterns on a pheasant's feathers help it to hide in grasses. Parrots' brightly coloured feathers make them easy to see.

Find the answers

Which animals have feathers?

Why are a flamingo's feathers pink?

golden pheasant

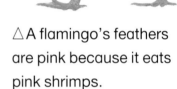

parrots

◁ A peacock spreads his tail feathers into a beautiful fan to attract a mate.

Beaks and bills

All birds have hard beaks, or bills. Birds' beaks give clues to what they eat. Sparrows have stubby, little bills for crushing seeds. Eagles have sharp, curved bills for tearing meat.

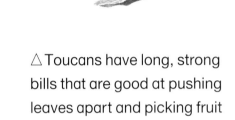

◁ Curlews have long, thin bills for poking into sand and mud.

△ Toucans have long, strong bills that are good at pushing leaves apart and picking fruit and nuts.

▷ Wrens have pointed beaks for snatching insects.

◁ Pelicans have a pouch of skin under their beaks to scoop up fish.

Make a bird beak card
Fold some card in half and cut a slit in middle. Fold back corners. Push folds inside out. Glue to a piece of card. Do not glue beak. Draw a bird's face around the beak. Open and close card to move beak.

Nests and eggs

Most birds build nests to protect their eggs. The nests must be hidden out of reach from their enemies.

Usually, nests are made with leaves, twigs and grasses. Other birds build their nests by pushing stones into a pile. When the female is ready, she lays her eggs. Then she sits on them, spreading her feathers to keep them warm, until her chicks hatch.

▽ Storks build a big, untidy nest of twigs, high up, away from their enemies.

stork

▽ The tailor bird makes a neat little nest by sewing leaves together.

tailor bird

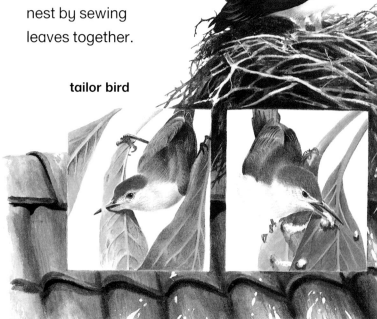

1

embryo

2

3   4

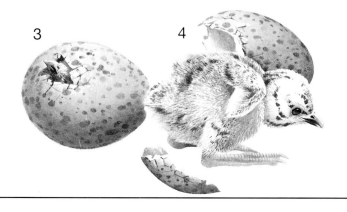

△ A bird's egg contains an embryo that grows into a chick. The chick gets bigger and bigger. When it is ready to hatch, it cracks the shell with a special part of its beak, called the egg-tooth, and crawls out.

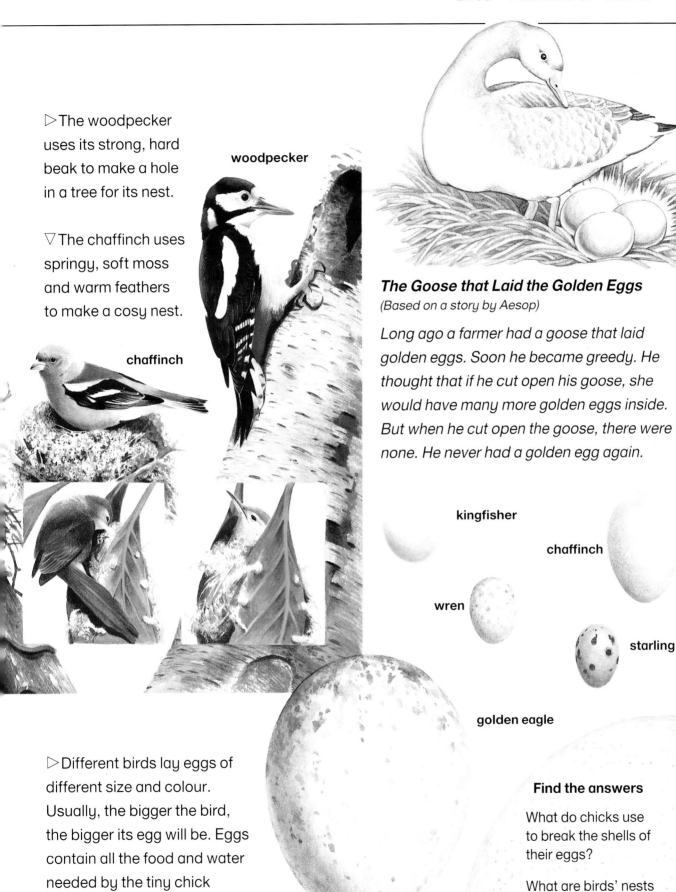

▷The woodpecker uses its strong, hard beak to make a hole in a tree for its nest.

woodpecker

▽ The chaffinch uses springy, soft moss and warm feathers to make a cosy nest.

chaffinch

The Goose that Laid the Golden Eggs
(Based on a story by Aesop)

Long ago a farmer had a goose that laid golden eggs. Soon he became greedy. He thought that if he cut open his goose, she would have many more golden eggs inside. But when he cut open the goose, there were none. He never had a golden egg again.

kingfisher

chaffinch

wren

starling

golden eagle

▷Different birds lay eggs of different size and colour. Usually, the bigger the bird, the bigger its egg will be. Eggs contain all the food and water needed by the tiny chick inside the shell.

Find the answers

What do chicks use to break the shells of their eggs?

What are birds' nests usually made from?

27

Flying hunters

Birds that hunt animals are called birds of prey. Some birds of prey soar high above the ground, using their excellent sight and hearing to spot any movement below them. When the bird finds its prey, it swoops silently for the kill.

▽ Most owls sleep in the day and hunt at night. This barn owl is taking a rat to its chicks.

talon

△ Eagles have long, sharp talons to catch their prey. They hunt during the day.

Why owls hoot
(A Scandinavian folk tale)

It was day when the king of the animals gave birds their songs. At night, when the owls awoke, all the songs had gone. Nearby a musician was playing "hoo-hoo" on his double-bass. So the owls copied that sound and used it as their song.

Swimmers and divers

Some birds spend a lot of their time in water. Most waterbirds have short, powerful legs with webbed feet, which they use as paddles. Some swim on top of the water, others dive beneath it. Often, birds that seem clumsy on land are skilful swimmers.

▷ Penguins use their wings as flippers when they swim.

Make a penguin

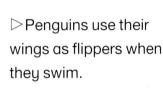

Copy the penguin shape onto card. Colour it in and cut it out. Cut out two yellow triangles for feet. Paint a cardboard tube black. When the paint is dry, stick the body and feet onto the cardboard tube.

△ The kingfisher perches by a stream. When it sees a fish, it dives into the water with folded wings. It grabs the fish with its strong, pointed beak.

What is a reptile?

Crocodiles, snakes, lizards, tortoises and turtles are all reptiles. Reptiles are cold-blooded animals. This means that they cannot keep their bodies warm in cold weather. They need lots of sunshine to keep warm, so most reptiles live in hot countries. Reptiles that live in cold countries sleep all winter and wake up in spring. This is called hibernation.

gila monster

△ Reptiles bask in the sun to get warm. If a reptile gets too hot, it hurries into the shade or into some cool water.

reptiles have
scaly skin

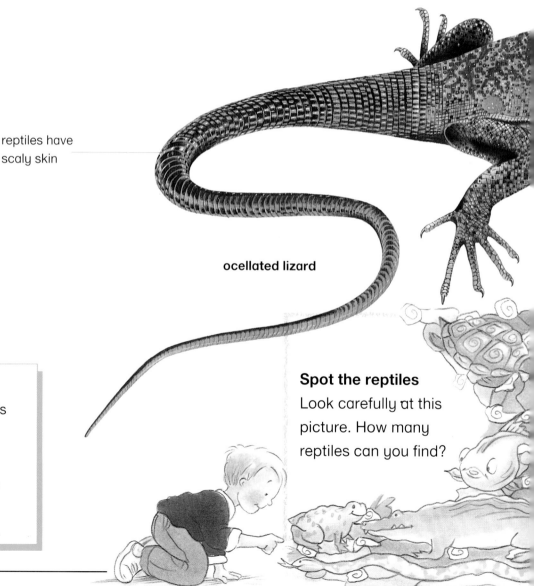

ocellated lizard

Word box
Warm-blooded animals keep themselves warm by eating.
Cold-blooded animals need heat from the sun to keep warm.

Spot the reptiles
Look carefully at this picture. How many reptiles can you find?

marine turtle

△ Some reptiles live longer than any other animal. Large turtles and tortoises can live for more than 100 years.

Find the answers

Is a crocodile a reptile?

How do reptiles get warm?

Are reptiles' eggs hard like birds' eggs?

◁ Geckos have sucker like pads on their feet. This helps them to run up walls when hunting for insects.

many reptiles are brightly coloured

▷ This king snake is hatching from its egg. Reptiles' eggs are not hard like birds' eggs, but soft and leathery.

▷ As it grows, a king snake will shed its skin. It has a brand new skin underneath. The snake rubs its head against something rough until the old skin splits open. Then the snake wriggles out.

31

Snakes

All snakes are meat-eaters. They can open their mouths very wide to swallow animals that are bigger than they are. Snakes do not chew their food, they swallow it whole. Some snakes use a poison called venom to kill their prey. When they bite, their sharp fangs inject venom into the animal.

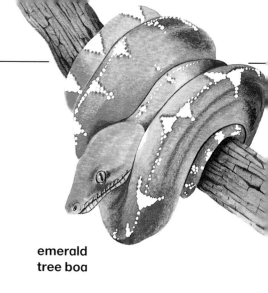

emerald tree boa

△Some snakes live in the trees. They coil around the branches.

▷Poisonous snakes often warn animals to keep away by hissing, spitting, or rattling their tails.

fang

rattlesnake

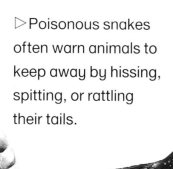

Find the answers

How do poisonous snakes warn off other animals?

How do anacondas kill their prey?

Do snakes chew their food?

▽Some snakes kill by coiling around an animal and squeezing it until it cannot breathe. Boa constrictors and pythons do this. The anaconda is a boa constrictor that lives near the water.

anaconda

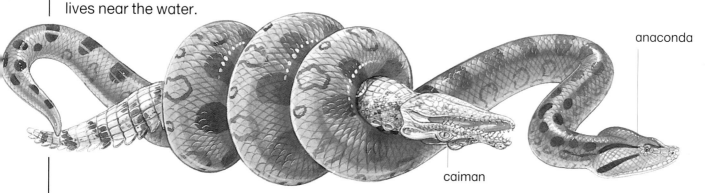

caiman

△ Snakes smell with their tongues, not their noses. This helps them track down things to eat.

▽ Cobras are poisonous. They spread out their necks to look bigger and more frightening.

cobra

Make a spiral snake
Draw a spiral inside a circle (like the one shown but much larger). Colour it in with bright colours and mark some eyes on the head in the centre. Cut along the line of the spiral. Attach string to the head and hang it up.

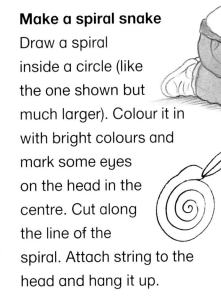

▽ The scarlet snake moves by looping its body and throwing its head forwards.

1   2   3

Chameleons

The chameleon is a lizard that lives in trees. It grips the branches with its tail and toes. A chameleon catches insects by shooting out its sticky tongue and pulling them into its mouth.

△ Chameleons are usually green or brown, but they can change colour to match their background. This is called camouflage, and it helps them to hide from their enemies.

△ Chameleons also turn dark when they are angry, and pale when they are afraid.

△ A chameleon's tongue is almost the same length as its body. It shoots out and in again very quickly.

Crocodiles

Crocodiles are large, fierce reptiles. Some are as big as six metres long. They live in rivers in hot countries, and are powerful swimmers. Crocodiles are good parents. They guard their eggs and look after the babies when they hatch.

△ When crocodiles are in water, they keep their eyes and nostrils above the surface so they can see and breathe.

Make snappy sweets
Add food colouring to a large chuhk of fondant icing (bought or home-made). Roll into sausages and flatten one end to make tails. Make legs and stick on. Use plain icing to make eyes and noses.

▽ With only their nostrils showing, crocodiles wait for animals that come to the river to drink. Then they seize their prey with their huge jaws.

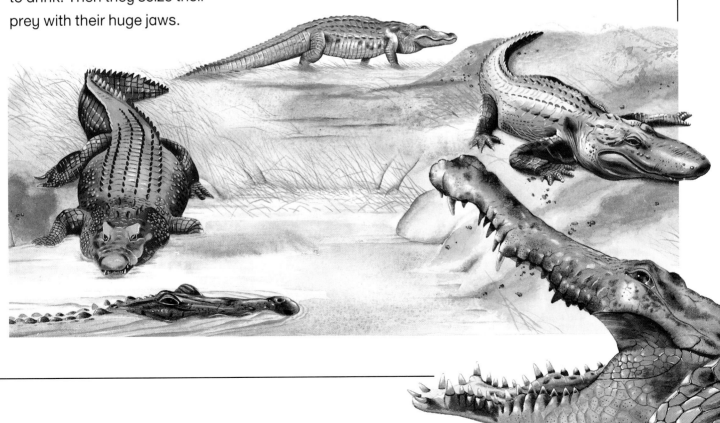

Turtles and tortoises

Turtles and tortoises are reptiles that have a hard shell covering their bodies. Because their shells are heavy, tortoises and turtles can only move slowly on land. A tortoise spends all its time on land. When it is in danger it can pull its head and legs into its shell. A turtle spends most of its time in the sea.

green turtle

Find the answers

What can tortoises do when they are in danger?

Where do turtles lay eggs?

△ Turtles might move slowly on land, but in the water they are fast swimmers. Turtles eat jellyfish and other sea animals, and seaweed too.

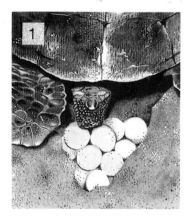

◁ Turtles lay their eggs on land. The green turtle digs a hole on the beach. She lays lots of eggs, covers them with sand and returns to the sea. When the babies hatch, they make for the sea. Many are eaten on the way by birds.

Make a tortoise puppet

Make a hole on each side of a paper bowl or tub. Stretch elastic through the holes and tie. Glue brown paper patches onto the tub to make the shell. Stick eyes on the middle finger of a glove to make a head. Wear the glove and thread the shell over your hand.

The Hare and the Tortoise
(A story by Aesop)

Have you heard the story of a hare who made fun of a tortoise for being so slow? They had a race. The hare was so sure he would win he went to sleep on the way, but the tortoise kept plodding on and won the race.

▷Tortoises eat leaves, fruit and grass. They have no teeth. Tortoises have a mouth like a beak with a hard bite.

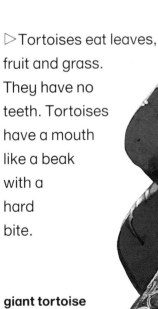

giant tortoise

What is an amphibian?

An amphibian is an animal that lives both in water and on land. Frogs, toads, newts and salamanders are amphibians. Amphibians lay their eggs in water, perhaps in a pond or stream. Amphibians cannot live in salt water, so there are none in the sea.

Find the answers

Where do tadpoles live?

What is an amphibian?

Is a newt an amphibian?

great crested newt

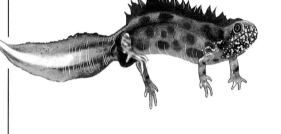

▷Newts and salamanders are amphibians. Unlike frogs or toads, they do not lose their tails when they grow up.

long-tailed salamander

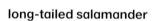

alpine salamander

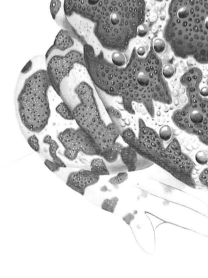

Word box
Amphibians are animals that spend part of their life in water and part on land.
Tadpoles turn into frogs or toads after losing their tails and developing legs.

frogs and toads have two strong back legs for jumping and swimming

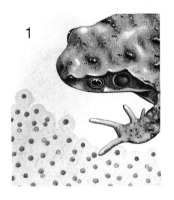

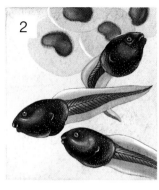

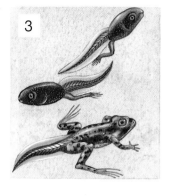

△ Female frogs lay hundreds of small eggs in water. The eggs hatch into tadpoles, with long tails. To start with, tadpoles only eat plants.

△ The tadpoles get bigger and begin to grow legs. Their tails shrink, and after about four months, the baby frogs can leave the water.

amphibians have two eyes that can see all around them

▽ Male frogs and toads puff up their throats with air and let out a big, loud croak.

reed frog

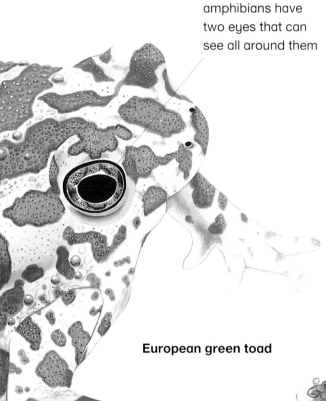

European green toad

Frog jumping race
Can you jump like a frog? Squat down and stretch your arms to the floor. Leap forward with a powerful jump. Have a frog race with your friends.

What is a fish?

A fish spends its whole life in water. Some fish live in the sea, and some in rivers and lakes. Their bodies are usually covered with scales.

Like all animals, fish need oxygen to live. We get oxygen from air, but fish get it from water. Water enters the fish's mouth and passes over its gills, which take in the oxygen. The water then goes out through gill slits.

◁ Most fish lay eggs, often thousands at a time. The eggs have no shells, and many are eaten by other fish. Only a few hatch.

▽ The butterflyfish has a big spot like an eye to confuse its enemies.

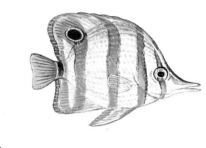

herring

a tail helps most fish push through water

scale

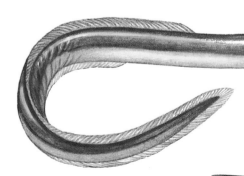

eel

The Little Mermaid
Hans Andersen wrote a story about a mermaid. Mermaids are imaginary sea creatures. They are like humans, but have a fish's tail instead of legs.

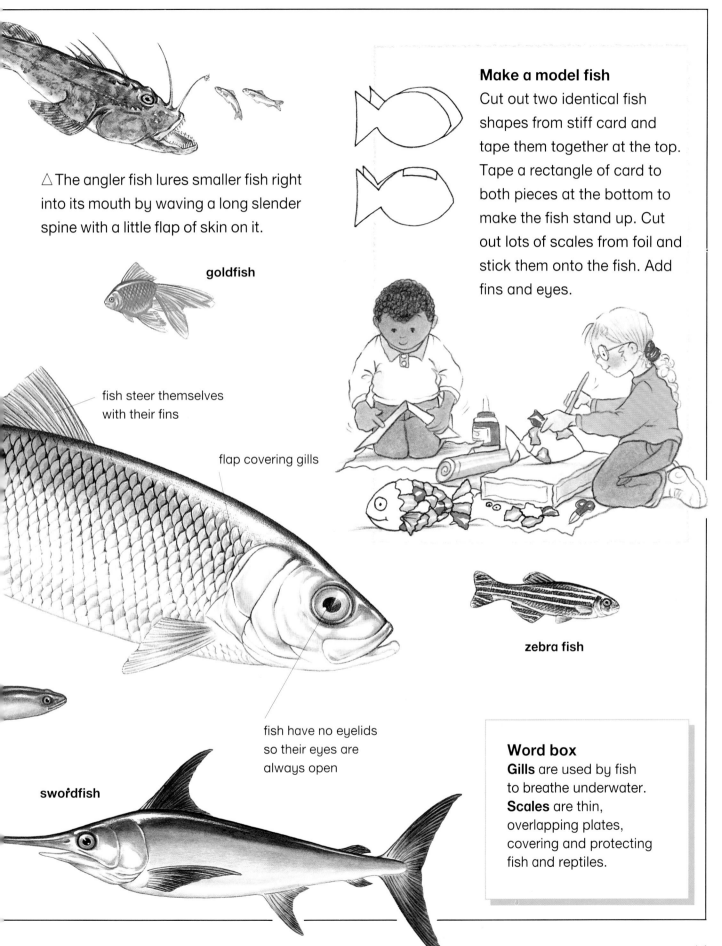

△ The angler fish lures smaller fish right into its mouth by waving a long slender spine with a little flap of skin on it.

goldfish

fish steer themselves with their fins

flap covering gills

Make a model fish
Cut out two identical fish shapes from stiff card and tape them together at the top. Tape a rectangle of card to both pieces at the bottom to make the fish stand up. Cut out lots of scales from foil and stick them onto the fish. Add fins and eyes.

zebra fish

fish have no eyelids so their eyes are always open

swordfish

Word box
Gills are used by fish to breathe underwater.
Scales are thin, overlapping plates, covering and protecting fish and reptiles.

41

Sharks

Some fish feed on plants in the water, and some feed on other fish. Sharks eat animals of any kind. They are fast swimmers and fierce hunters. Sharks have a good sense of smell, which helps them find animals to eat. Unlike most other fish, sharks have to keep swimming all the time or they sink.

Find the answers

What do sharks eat?

What is a mermaid's purse?

How do sharks find animals to eat?

▷Some sharks lay eggs in cases. These cases are called mermaids' purses.

mermaid's purse

▽These two great white sharks are hunting a dolphin. Great whites are known as man-eaters because they sometimes attack people.

Salmon

Salmon have an amazing life. They hatch in rivers, and then swim down to the sea. When they are ready to breed, the adult salmon swim all the way back from the sea to the rivers where they were born.

start

Follow the salmon's journey to the river
Use your finger to find the right way for the salmon to get back to the river.

finish

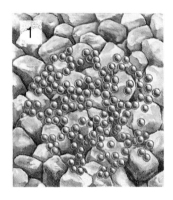

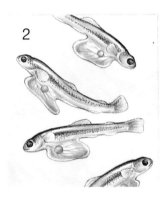

△ The female salmon lays her eggs in the river where she was born. When the eggs hatch, the babies are called fry.

▽ Adult salmon swim upstream to reach the river where they were born. They often have to leap up rushing waterfalls on the way.

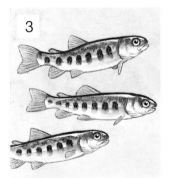

△ The young salmon live and grow in the river for over two years. When they are large enough, they swim down to the sea.

What is an insect?

Insects have six legs. Their bodies have a hard outer case called an exoskeleton. Every insect's body has three parts: a head, a thorax or middle and an abdomen at the back.

Most insects can fly. Usually, insects have two pairs of wings. All flies, however, have only one pair of wings.

Insects are often brightly coloured to warn other animals not to eat them because they taste nasty.

△ This ladybird has two pairs of wings. The front wings are hard, and they cover the delicate back wings when the ladybird is not flying.

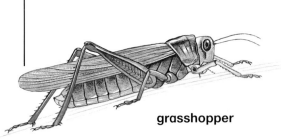

grasshopper

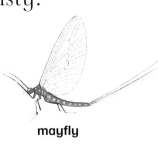

mayfly

an insect's legs and wings are attached to the thorax

housefly

Word box
Antennae are the two feelers on the heads of small creatures, such as insects.
Metamorphosis is the complete change that happens to some creatures' bodies before they become adults.

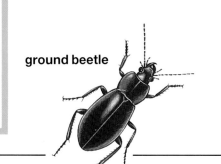

ground beetle

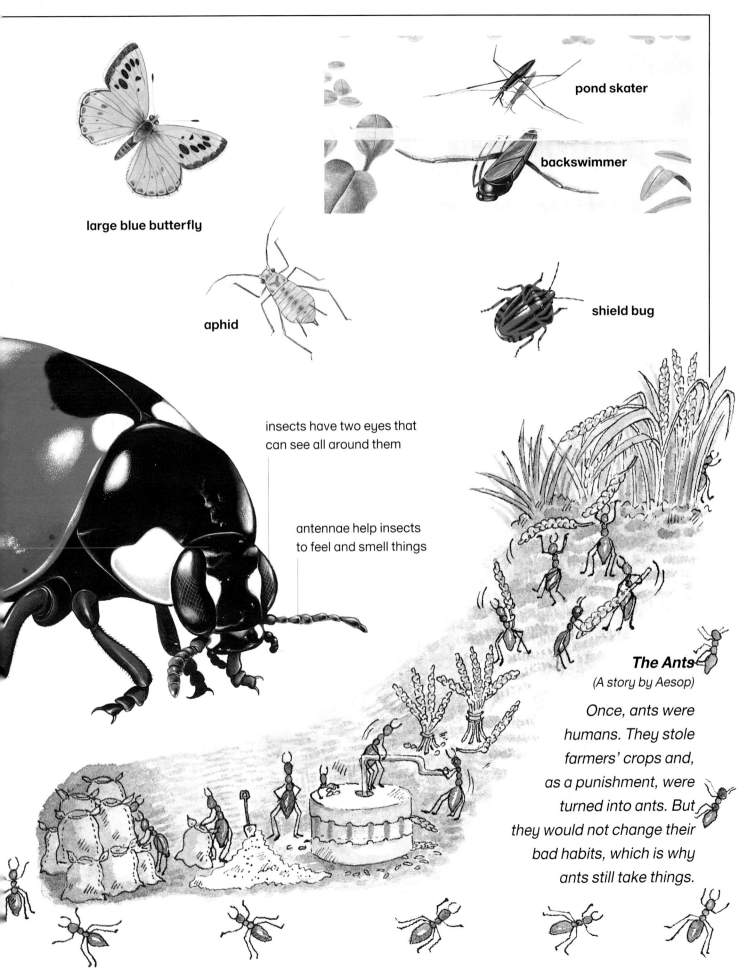

pond skater

backswimmer

large blue butterfly

aphid

shield bug

insects have two eyes that can see all around them

antennae help insects to feel and smell things

The Ants
(A story by Aesop)

Once, ants were humans. They stole farmers' crops and, as a punishment, were turned into ants. But they would not change their bad habits, which is why ants still take things.

Butterflies

Some of the most beautiful insects are butterflies. Their wings are covered with tiny, overlapping scales which give the wings their bright colours.

Butterflies, like many insects, go through several different stages before becoming adults. This change in their bodies is called metamorphosis.

△ The swallowtail butterfly lays eggs on a plant that her babies will be able to eat.

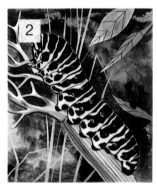
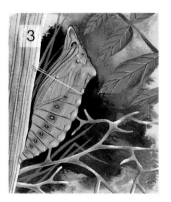
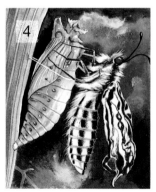

△ A caterpillar hatches out of each butterfly egg. Caterpillars eat a lot and grow quickly. The caterpillar turns into a chrysalis. Out of this crawls a beautiful butterfly.

Make butterfly prints

Fold a piece of paper in half.

 Open it up and put spots of paint on one side.

Refold and press down. Open out. When dry, paint a body and two antennae to complete a butterfly picture.

A wasps' nest

Some insects, such as wasps, live in large groups. There may be 8,000 wasps in just one nest. In each giant family, the wasps work together and depend on each other to survive.

In spring, the queen wasp builds the nest. She scrapes wood from trees, chews it up and mixes it with her saliva to make each cell or room in the nest.

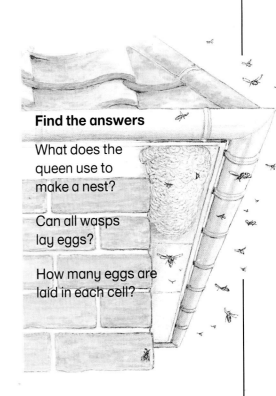

Find the answers

What does the queen use to make a nest?

Can all wasps lay eggs?

How many eggs are laid in each cell?

The queen wasp lays one egg in each of the cells she has made. The eggs hatch into grubs and are fed on insects. The grubs grow into adults and leave the cells.

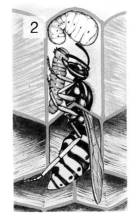

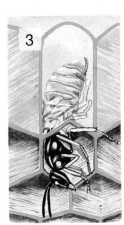

△ When the new adults hatch, most of them take over the nest building and find food for the queen and her next batch of grubs. These are called workers. Only the queen wasp lays eggs.

Molluscs

Molluscs are animals with soft bodies. Many are protected by a hard shell. Those with shells either have one shell or two shells hinged together. Many molluscs live in water. Land molluscs are covered with slime to keep their bodies moist.

octopus

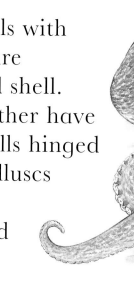

△ The octopus is a mollusc without a shell. It has eight long arms to catch animals to eat.

sea slug

queen conch

garden snail

△ Many molluscs can pull their bodies back inside their shells to protect themselves.

scallop

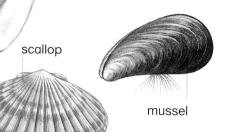

mussel

◁ Molluscs with two shells live in water. They filter tiny bits of food from the water.

Word box
Molluscs have soft bodies and they usually have hard shells made of chalk.
Crustaceans have close-fitting hard cases that form their skeletons. These cases need to be shed as the animal grows.

Make a shell creature
Collect lots of different shells. Glue them together to make creatures. Draw on eyes.

Crustaceans

The animals here are called crustaceans. They all have a tough, crusty covering, or case. They have to shed this as they grow bigger. Many crustaceans have long antennae to help them find their way around. Crabs, lobsters and prawns are crustaceans.

lobster

▷ Lobsters and crabs have huge claws for protecting themselves, and for picking up food.

antenna

hermit crab

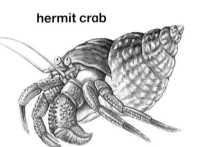

△ The hermit crab lives inside an old shell. As it grows, it must move to a bigger shell.

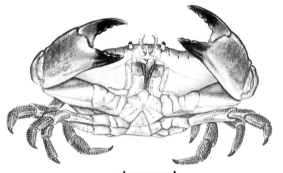

shore crab

◁ Crabs and lobsters have ten legs and scuttle over the sea bed. Some are good swimmers too.

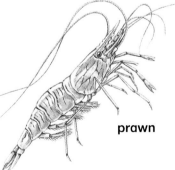

◁ Prawns have ten legs for walking, and more for swimming.

prawn

▽ Crabs move by walking sideways.

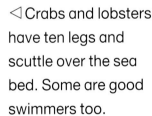

Find the answers

Where do hermit crabs live?

How many legs do crabs and lobsters have?

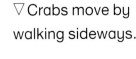

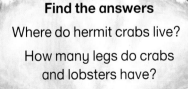

Spiders

Spiders are animals with eight legs. Most spiders catch their food by building webs of silk. Insects get caught in the silk and the spider eats them. As they grow bigger, spiders grow new skins and shed their old ones.

most spiders have two rows of four eyes, which makes eight eyes altogether

spiders pull threads of silk from tiny spinnerets

house spider

Make a pom-pom spider
Wind wool around two discs of card with large holes in the middle. When finished, push four long pipe-cleaners through the middle to make legs. Cut the wool around the outside and tie the pom-pom securely between the discs. Remove the card and fluff up. Bend the pipe-cleaners to look like legs and stick on eyes.

△ Many spiders can walk up walls because their feet have hairy pads for extra grip. A spider does not get stuck in its own web because it walks only on the spokes of the web and these are not sticky.

A garden spider's web

△ First the spider spins a bridge thread.

△ Then it adds spokes.

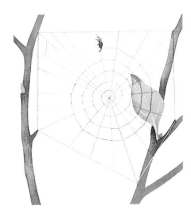

△ It finishes with a spiral of silk.

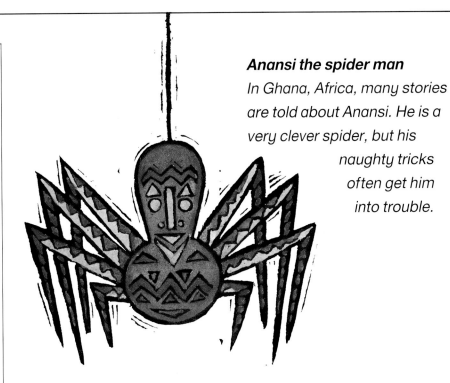

Anansi the spider man

In Ghana, Africa, many stories are told about Anansi. He is a very clever spider, but his naughty tricks often get him into trouble.

Find the answers

How many legs does a spider have?

How can a spider walk up walls?

△ When a fly is caught in a web, the spider can feel it along the threads. The spider bites the fly with poisonous fangs, wraps it in silk and keeps it to eat later.

Worms

Earthworms are strange-looking animals. They do not have eyes, ears or legs. They spend their lives under the ground, tunnelling. Tiny bristles help them grip as they wriggle along. At night, earthworms come up to look for dead leaves. They pull the leaves down into their burrows to eat in safety.

Find the answers

What do worms eat?

What are worm casts?

Do worms have eyes?

Make a worm doorstop
Cut off a leg from an old pair of children's tights. Fill it with scrunched up newspaper, old tights or bits of material. Tie a knot in the end. Stick on eyes, nose and wool hair.

▽ Earthworms swallow soil while tunnelling. They eat dead plants and animal remains in the soil. The leftovers are pushed up above ground, making small heaps called worm casts.

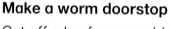

worm cast

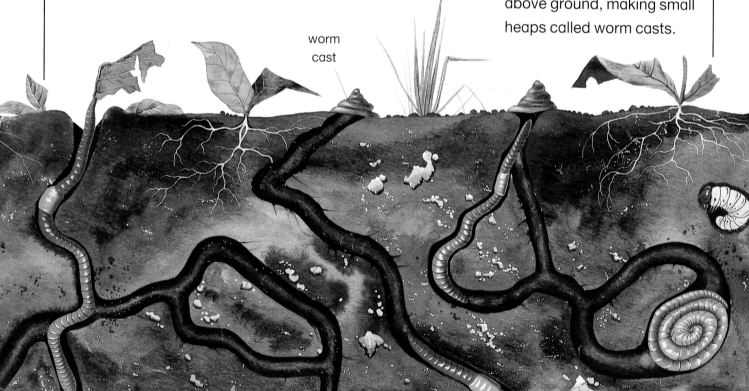

Index

This index will help you to find out where you can read information about a subject. It is in alphabetical order. Each section is under a large letter of the alphabet. A main entry and its page numbers are printed in **dark**, or **bold**, letters. This is where you will find the most information. Below a main entry, there may be a second list. This shows other places in the book where you can find further information on your subject.